A HABIT OF LANDSCAPE

poems by

Shelley Armitage

Finishing Line Press
Georgetown, Kentucky

A HABIT OF LANDSCAPE

Copyright © 2023 by Shelley Armitage
ISBN 979-8-88838-370-4 First Edition
All rights reserved under International and Pan-American Copyright Conventions. No part of this book may be reproduced in any manner whatsoever without written permission from the publisher, except in the case of brief quotations embodied in critical articles and reviews.

Also by Shelley Armitage

Reading into Photography
John Held, Jr.: Illustrator of the Jazz Age
Women's Work: Essays in Cultural Studies
Kewpies and Beyond: The World of Rose O'Neill
Wind's Trail: The Early Life of Mary Austin
This Dancing Ground of Sky: Poems of Peggy Pond Church
Bones Incandescent: The Pajarito Journals of Peggy Pond Church
Walking the Llano: A Texas Memoir of Place

Publisher: Leah Huete de Maines
Editor: Christen Kincaid
Cover Art: Rick Dingus
Author Photo: Greg Conn
Cover Design: Elizabeth Maines McCleavy

Order online: www.finishinglinepress.com
also available on amazon.com

Author inquiries and mail orders:
Finishing Line Press
P. O. Box 1626
Georgetown, Kentucky 40324
U. S. A.

Table of Contents

I.

Counting Cattle with the Fathers 1
In Aunt Alice's Root Cellar 3
Glidden's Barbed Wire, ca. 1873 5
Graphite Dreams 6
Eighteen Cedar Waxwings 7
Bellwether 8
Plainsong 9
Little Foxes 11
Antelope and I 12

II.

Cecil 17
Let There Be Stones 18
Trace 20
Friendship 21
Requiem 22
Purple Iris 23
Invitro Bandstand 24
Demeter's Revenge 26
Mimosa 27
Palimpsest 28
Languages Lost 29

III.

What Beauty Does 33
Arizona Cypress 34
Gathering 35
A Butterfly Once Landed 36
Removal 37
Strange Fruit 39
She (Un)Names Them 40
Blue Heron 42

Acknowledgments 44

For Deborah

Habit: archaic. To inhabit. [Middle Engish (h)*abit*, from Old French, from Latin *habitus*, from the past participle of *habere*, to hold.]

Habitat: Latin it dwells (the first word in Latin descriptions of plant and animal species in old natural histories), third person singular present indicative of *habitare*, to inhabit.

I.

Counting Cattle with the Fathers

We find them, tails to the wind.
They eye us with cold curiosity
and the dull hope of hay.
They distance themselves as we
amble by.

We go in the "four-banger" pickup,
the old four-wheel-drive with no heater.
We are counting the cattle,
in the six degree morning
my father, my grandfather, and I.

Father says the heater works.
He dogs the temperature gauge
turns the blower on full blast
in bull-headed persistence
while I stoically wish to turn tail.

Hell, it's cold, I think but don't say it
It's his time to be right as it was his father's
who drove his '46 Kaiser axle-deep in snow
to castrate by the astrological sign.
Now his son cuts when the knife is sharp.

This is the faith of my fathers living still
in spite of the market, the weather, or Uncle Sam.
Grandfather, the departed one, who now whispers
in ghost breaths, swore by the almanac, at the soil bank.
The other has lived long enough to see the blood come to a daughter.

It has been this way with fathers and sons,
counting buffalo, counting coup, counting cattle.
But I am the daughter now rightly come
to this dominion of grass and fathers
and pissing in the wind.

Down in the draw all are stone
womb and semen, hoof and horn.
For a moment we are all frozen together in time,
except for one steer who says *tomorrow* with
his dry humping.

(Once when I was five
I saw two dogs do it and asked my daddy.
He lit a cigarette, I ventured it was a circus trick
and we drove on.)

But oh, my dumb darlings
how you flourish in spite of us.

Oh, my dumb darlings
I can't help it.
I have a mother's love for you
though I will pen you, brand you, alter you.
It's all for your own good.

Together we count one too many
even knowing Ferdinand the Bull is gone again.
He jumps fences with his green notions
leaving nothing but hide behind.
One day he'll be just plain Ferdinand.

But old bull, you're the key.
I will inherit this, this counting
and two visionary ghosts to say
you missed that one
in the place where a rock is a calf.

In Aunt Alice's Root Cellar

Down here, down under
I admit to allusions.
Like a too-large grave
this cellar has an appetite
for bones, mine included.

The cats race down the wooden stairs
entering the region of who-knows-what
of their nine lives. They are present-
oriented in their hide and seek.
They have only their bodies as history.

I've meant to clean this cellar
since moving here,
inheritor of your old farmhouse
and your sixty-odd years
of random storage.

Instead for years I simply hang
my molting onions, string by string
wintering over from your old seed beds—
what one puts store by.

Now, like Carter, I enter this tomb expectant, fearful.
Just the other day a melting cardboard box
(there are leaks here in snow and rainy seasons)
revealed a waterdog with heart
and viscera pressed outside.

Such fragile skin! That day I found a treasure:
three aging quilts, whip-stitched by my great grandmother
who died at age 102. Somehow the warped
and mildewed trunk seems to hold the magic
of her withered fingers, her miraculous eyes.

Aunt, you have left lamps from the 1940s,
their ceramic Oriental pink flowers a recent antiquity.
And canned pickles, aging jams. Discarded books,
Hugh Miller, Katherine Morris, *The Guide*
to the Castration of Domestic Animals.

Much life is contained in these musty dirt walls.
I choose to keep your shells from some far-off seacoast,
pink and sandy still. Your husband's old fishing pole,
his cracking wicker basket, seed packets to be conjured
next spring.

Out on these dry plains there was a vision of paradise.
Taking these steps one more time, in this scarab of self,
I realize death is making one light enough to leave.
It's not the weight of spirit that encumbers us
but the load of our unshed skins.

Glidden's Barbed Wire, ca. 1876

Those whose small teeth

                         bite space, chew raw hides
               clot with raw hopes

Those whose shaggy notions

                         violate ownership, section lines
                             eschew barbs, pressure space

Those who would graze on the other side

                                 straight into the mouth of desire heave

    Somewhere on them are bald dreams.

Graphite Dreams

Plains a blank page
smudge of chalky gray
printed in scuffs of caliche road
winding behind, sifting above
blue masked, colored, then blown away
replaced by desolation, by trudging.
What surfaces as mirage
imagined, penciled down:
twelve pronghorns prancing
stop then flee the prairie's grasp
footfalls breaking open a poem—
words not there before.

Eighteen Cedar Waxwings

Not thirteen ways,
maybe more—eighteen?
I do like the sound of it:
Eighteen cedar waxwings
in the pine tree in the north yard.

Like museum pieces—

> *The stiff custodian in the shadows*
> *at the Wax Museum in Anaheim.*
> *I thought he was watching us,*
> *a sort of brooding figure*
> *in the background*
> *who could sweep us up*
> *and out.*
> *He could find our gum*
> *stuck in the wrong places*
> *kidnap, murder us,*
> *while our parents strolled*
> *from Lincoln to Reagan.*
> *But he too was a wax figure,*
> *never flinching (and neither did we).*

Standing that still
I look at you,
black topnotch,
ochre flash. (You do fidget.)

I think of your looping
movements just moments ago
seen through my kitchen window—
what drew me out.

And now we are locked
in our looking
in a world wound down
neither willing to melt away.

Bellwether

We wake within medieval walls lime-washed marked by the Knights of Templar,
an old bull ring at one end of town, Igreju Matriz de Santa Maria de Castelo church
at the other. At midnight we race back and forth so our backs press
against vibrating cathedral walls as the bell strikes twelve.

Oh, to feel time in this place inhabited by Celts, Romans, Visigoths, Moors,
on this border with Spain, on this slope above the Alentejo plain.

We stay in a writer's house set deep in the ground, schist walls studded
with books and crockery. Above ground the upper story windows frame clouds
so that we wake to a sky struck open by the bell of a ram leading his flock
down to pasture. With each beat we follow; we float above histories.

Brochures recommend local ceramics for souvenirs, but we seek out
the village metalsmith to find a hammered brass bell strapped in leather.
Carneiro guiador, the bellwether, the smith offers, *does not predict.
His chiming describes where he has been, not where he is going.*

Cast in memories not our own, with no sheep at home,
still our wonder echoes like a clapper before the next strike.

Plainsong

My call might scare
the *bejesus* out of you
so I'll quietly soar here above
passing for a buzzard—
a humiliation—except for how
the silence tugs at my tail.

Your Border Patrol
Your Google Earth
Your National Geographic photographers
objectify me.

But I see you.

A mile away I distinguish my prey,
prairie dog, black tailed jack rabbit,
occasional pronghorn.
Golden eagles are known for
our sharp eyesight, our size.

I eye that seed cap of yours
and your partner's red bandanna,
human detritus prized among the prickly barbed wire,
mesquite sticks, antlers, ripe yucca, all woven—
how I make my nest.

You could read a long ancestral ecology
from my nest, reworked sometimes
for over 100 years, aerial dendrochronology
the rings up to five feet in diameter,
the nest over six feet tall,
locked into ledges, a cliff face,
nestled sky.

You marvel.
You sigh.
You measure.

You photograph.

From these heights
I see you as part of the horizontal
green of the spring's seep,
the rattlesnake's brown coil,
the llano's endless yellow.

You wonder at the origins of the pictographs nearby.
Yes, you say that blue one on the overhang is an angel.
But it is a shaman and the spirits are unhappy
with your ancestors who have camped here,
scratching their names.

I can see where the Comancheros followed arroyos
where the basalt cliffs break into plains
the wandering Spanish ever lost
the migration of Pueblo peoples and pronghorns.
You walk upright among equivocal patterns.

Kyrie, kyrie, I call.
Leave that nice ball cap behind.

Little Foxes

Light's ellipsis
       burnt   caramel

              slight
A rustle felt not

       heard
Tall grasses bend,

   weeds too

In the barn loft   radar ears
   the framed window rotting

They pass while I sleep
   hear me in the bathroom
       the kitchen

       the dining room

      each view I

        haunt

              spiked

              sound.

Antelope and I

You see me—of course—before I see you.
But then as I walk a sage fringed trail
up the draw and down, something—
a shared animal presence?—
makes me look west: see you.

                        Even at seventy-five yards
                        your bold white chest,
                        radiant exception to the plains
                        gone dun, cures my
                        nearsightedness.
You, on the other hand, can spot movement at three miles away.

Pronghorn, *kwahada, antilocapra americana,*
neither antelope nor deer,
               (your closest living cousin, the giraffe)
ancestry assures you persist with
hollowed hairs, your antifreeze for winter,
camouflaged coat, butterscotch stripes and all.

Side set eyes catch worlds in their orbs
long lashes like sunshades.
Nervous, curious—your Pleistocene genes
still bolt, then stand.

Now this is fossil fuel: at speeds of fifty miles an hour
your ancient bloodline remembers ghosts of grasslands
chaparral   cacti. You disappear, sliding under on your knees
mocking the wisdom of barbed wire.

                        But I am exotic am I not?
                        My old checkered farm coat, sagging sleeves,
                        baggy warm-ups, a whiff of acrid humanness,
                        the unwashed best tolerated upwind.
                        I am held at a distance by your gaze.

We used to talk to animals—
or was it animals talked to us—
until evolutionary changes in the trachea
made one claim superiority over the other.

But if you were the carnivore
I would offer myself up
even as you did to the old Zuni

> *line to the heart*
> *prayer over horns*

Instead, I can only say in a stillness
beyond thought:
> *I would be the grass before you.*

II

Cecil

An African lion popular in a Zimbabwe park because he allowed humans to come near, Cecil was killed by a trophy hunter in 2021 after being lured away from his protected sanctuary. Named for the African explorer Cecil Rhodes, Cecil had been radio collared as part of an important study for years.

The first time stung a night into being
the dart brought dreams of impala
sotted in drink their tails still as death
near the old mudhole.

Awake, he roamed free and even came close—
without consequence—to those two-legged deer,
the kind who, in erect and awkward scampers,
turned from their bush beating when he returned stare.

They had collared him but no leash.

This time, though, something was different:
Two pale deer followed the black leaders.
This time a sting tore his heart.

King of beasts, the stalkers called him.
But in the end he was just plain Cecil:
tufts of hair, tarnished mane, stilled bone
and gut after all. Nothing exotic.

Stuffed, he will preside over their dinners
subject of several courses of braggadocio and such.
But no matter what cutlery, what fine china or aged wine
it is they—they, they, they—
who are the kings of beasts.

Let There Be Stones

Stones ache

stones cry

just ask the desert

after a storm

stones rejoice

shout from the mountaintop

(The Comanches beat a huge boulder
with their lances, a big boulder for war
instructions. They called it Speaking Rock.)

Stones gather no moss

that is, rolling downhill

until they hit what miners call

the angle of repose

Stones age

as in a stone's age

or the Stone Age

just a stone's throw away.

My stones ache, they congregate

ten mm in the lower right kidney

no downhill for them

Blasted they scatter

like milkweed

no, sand

to pass another way

sifting into landfills

beginning again

Trace

With a curve of the tail—ermine lifted—you reigned over a kingdom bereft of rats
It was l935, your Sunday comics humor an upright droll

with your assistants (themselves two pussycats, but smaller)
carrying your uplifted train, the procession a striped delight: Pussycat Princess.

Why do I think of you when I see the local roadrunner
(*Geococcys californianus*) tack to and fro on the desert roads?

It's the tail, a ballast, a rudder,
balance a throwback to the dinosaurs.

My own showed up on the X ray, a tiny coccyx crack from a fall
healed over to add yet another bump to what was once a tail.

Vestigial they called it, a useless footprint, a trace.
But it caused chronic arthritis—an evolutionary ache—

restored a sensate memory of equilibrium, animal to animal
of how kin we are in our fur and boots.

Friendship

We shared a couple of red-necked boys
who stomped their boots to a western two-step
near a wind-gutted arroyo on the Canadian River
tent top dance, hot summer night, sticky
armpits the color of the fading sky.
We were on college break, no real boyfriends.
These two would have to do.
You'd left this little hometown of yours
famous for its sandy soil peaches
the year you went off to college leaving
you high school boyfriend and his dull ambitions behind.
He scrambled the letters on the local movie marquee
to read: *Jamie sucks.* Pretty embarrassing in this
little bible-toting West Texas town.
You told these stories at college. (We giggled, told ours.)
So when you broke your leg playing
pick-up basketball, we were all speechless,
your paling expression we'd never seen.
I shouldered you to my Beetle—another dance—
and said: *Jamie, I'm here for you.*
But at the doctor's office when he jerked
that baby into place, I fainted dead away,
making my way into another of your stories.

Requiem

For the feather—quail, dove?—along the trail.
For the touch—light as—lingering there.
My thigh, your car, the door, your hand

not here, not again, your wife, my friend.
Mottled, whisper proof, arched against ribald winds
fragile, yet built for flight, earth bound, heaven sent

Whose were you? Before the fox, before the pale?
When I saw you at the conference that last time
you crooked a finger, I obeyed.

I crossed the room to sit beside you, stumbled slightly—
your knee, my hand—before I learned you were caught
clipped wings, pressed jeans, in that landscape of forgetting.

Death by remembrance:
blood-tipped quill—that afterlife—writing here.

Purple Iris

Torqued   furled
    minute by minute

unsheathed   cusp of head
       nodding   mouth breached

gathered in rows below
          open windows   a small-town church

    made more   sanctuary   as you peek
  showering
        musk
            colors

   and
when done

                leave a stigmata to come

Invitro Bandstand

I remember your heartbeat—
(do you remember mine?)

and that Riviera supper club
full of GI's looking for a good time

You were no good time girl
not in that sense

But your heart raced as we danced
didn't we—cheek to cheek

me, in your swaying belly
what a ride that was.

You were a little old for the jitterbug
what I would have liked

It was 1946 after all, so you
held tight to *Stella by Starlight*

I Wonder Who's Kissing Her Now?
Open the Door, Richard

Never mind that was not his name
the army Major who retreated once

the letter came: *there's a baby on the way.*
He did write back and asked about your health

And by the way, he said,
I am married.

He always brought me flowers,
you said, *complimented my hair.*

Even today I can sway, remembering the lyrics
to those old songs—second stanzas too—

heard before I was born
your belly button my own Bose headphone.

You carried me alone
delivered me to a different beat

hands cupped in supplication
some *Fascinating Rhythm.*

It Had to Be You
just *You, the Night and the Music*

Dancing in the Dark
My Sweet Embraceable You.

Demeter's Revenge

You, oleander, are poison, despite your beauty
fake pink   and ruddy bloom.
Promised, full bushed   prolific
your seduction should caution:
Look, don't touch.
You could kill a child, for godsakes.
So do not tempt my sweet Persephone
herself plucked   ripped away so hungry
spirited to that madman's nether land.

O truth, O justice, what would that be?
A dose of global warming
or the more polite, Climate Change?
I've rocked Polar bears, after all—
reduced them to skin and bones.
Zeus, and everyone else knows
I will have justice for my baby girl.

Yes, she sucked sweet the pomegranate seeds
But who can deny a young woman's hunger?
Not Hades. Not Zeus. Not her mother.

Perhaps a mother's love would grant
twelve months of sunshine.
But that would mean overripe pomegranates
falling from the branch,
that would mean you   oleander   would reseed
to tempt again.

Mimosa

Mike told me about his daughter, Susan. She scraped her cheek on a Mimosa limb while playing and tore the skin. While it was healing she became obsessed with the scab, like children do. Each time she put a washcloth on it, it would stick to the cloth and come off. There would be a new scab. Eventually, Susan scarred her face. Mike didn't notice the process; he never realized the coming result. The scar, he says, is a loss. The face will never be the same. (The daughters, he reasons—the younger one, two, Susan, five—are different anyway.)

Their skin: a manifold weeping
Their eyes: the world wound down
Their voices: a lemon-sliced speaking

Never again the cheek's pure apogee
Never again the seamless skin

The coloring book, a waxwork
The doll, a monument of straw

It is said that once Michelangelo worked with the stone and found what pattern it possessed, he stopped sculpting. The father takes the girl to the Mimosa tree. He plucks a blossom and offers to powder pink her piqued face. Then, when he says he will cut down the tree, she cries.

This is the way of discovering flaws.

Palimpsest

I bite the head off
a small figure
(human?) and eat it
Goya-like.

My lover
tells me she's
leaving me for her
boyfriend (go figure)
and she does it with a sneer.

My mother (long gone)
chastens me
from across the room:
Your slip is showing
(I don't wear one.)

It's a restless night—
maybe the broccoli in the
too-late night dinner.
At an hour when the Dalai Lama awakens
to new understandings
I toss instead

What I'd hoped would come in lines
in my dreams
comes in fragments—
a mouse hole with lips

But forever Mother:
It's always good to hear your voice
your precise sentences from the other side.

Languages Lost

Adopted
basalt, repaginated
creosote scratching
down the already
evicted image
from some past
gradually evolved
high above on
igneous escarpments
jagged walls
kindred spirits
light skips by
moments in time
now present
Ozymandias in our desert
plumed serpent/goggle eyed
quiet of soul
risen pentimento
solace, chipped
twilight culture in
undulating lines of
vectored diamonds.
Why these petroglyphs
X-rays won't tell
you and I know only
A: Shiwi will. *

*Zuni

III.

What Beauty Does

Two trees, in a stand of five, arthritic
they call them when knotted that way.
Immigrant (Chinese or Siberian), invasive
you're called, seeds spawn in worldly
dispersal. Amber roots survive alkali
soils; mottled gray bark a leathery rivulet,
leaves, fishbone veined, clutch air.
You may be sixty years old, or more,
an epidermal knuckle; a pucker permanently hinged.
What of beauty defined this way?
I'd like to think you two did the tango—
one rooted in the other—or a florid
folk dance, maybe a fox trot, a dance of the hours.
Underground, fibrous skirts a twirl sheltered pain—
the drought years, beetles, an inevitable rotting core.
You stand upright among humbled grasses.
So entwined we'd like to be
holding hands like trees.
Modest their unseen love affair
until one dies and the other,
once so leafed and full of life
now, just this spring, stands bare.

Arizona Cypress

*They'll never be tall enough
to shade your grave,* he teased,
even as he drove the shovel blade deeper.
That was forty years ago, dad
your 6'3 frame shadowed them, spindly
Arizona Cypress said to resist drought
said to be short-lived. We planted thirteen
in the fence row. Now I'm just five years younger
than your age when you died buried
in our small-town prairie cemetery
rippled blue gramma, semaphore side oats
flowing a sunny September day—no trees.
How I like to look out the back window
—best near sunset—at the row of them, dancers
in the Texas wind, peeled bark glowing at sixty feet
waiting for me.

Gathering

No ceremony of sandwich
No pal of the desk
    I stand here ironing
    Or something like that
Memory cares
Muscles remember
    That synapse of roses
    That purple glass vase
Thorns a right of way
Pricking awake
other days when you were here
    a gardener, a caregiver
    tending the peace petals
gathering for her
    whose grave   later
      became a bed of roses.

A Butterfly Once Landed

A butterfly once landed on my brother's nose.
There they were, Roy R. and Mourning Cloak
at the Houston Botanical Gardens.
He had a checkered western shirt on

with fake Mother-of-Pearl snap down pockets.
He'd asked his sons to take him, compensation
for not being able to dip into his bucket list.
Too late.

They had so much in common!
Nymphalis antiope and *multiple myeloma*.
Both wore black wingtips.
Both were on oxygen.

He did look a bit like Eustace Tilley, my wry brother,
his head tipped that fey way, the black
butterfly balancing, though he had never read
a page of the *New Yorker*, never noticed the cover.

Mourning Cloak, you are so long lived
(for a butterfly) —ten to twelve
months—another commonality
what sweetness attracts.

Removal

No wonder I hunkered down
in your gardening shed that day—
the day of your funeral—
comforted by shovels, clumps of dirt
dried fast, your calico bonnet hanging near.
Without you, I turn to chemicals.
The wart on my hand slowly disappears,
no miracle peeling back its future.
Your touch, your healing touch—
and now you—gone.
What was it Mother said?
That the secret is passed from mother
to daughter, like a prayer.
I believed. I believed.

The secret came from your grandmother
more sepia now, aging as the photograph ages,
marked on the back, "Grandma Long."
Whose handwriting? Her identity surely more
than that, the wife of a Methodist circuit rider.
Was he home much, that traveling man?
The one who changed her name, removed her
with his history while he stayed safe within family,
a tiny, weathered psalm book with his name inscribed—
the saddlebag's snug fit. *Abide with me.*

Her name I never found
no matter what circuits searched,
what rolls I checked: North Carolina,
Oklahoma, southern Illinois, Texas.
But in the photograph, she is sternly present,
western dress, tight lace collar, prim buttons.
Deep-set eyes make steely sparks against a skin
the color of the dirt floor in her granddaughter's shed.

You, grandmother, who soothed wounds—
the green thumb, the herbalist's touch—I last saw
through the steam of a local cleaners, where,
in the back room, your hands pressed wrinkles
from some stranger's long pants.
The secret was to be passed from
mother to daughter, like a prayer.
Though I am adopted, still I long to hear
the whisper in the blood.

Strange Fruit

What do I know, here in the garden, as I watch
birds in updraft dodge the fields at night
like developing prints, their shadow and act.

What did my mother know as she witnessed
the last hanging in Collingsworth County, Texas—
a white man, framed some said, pleading his innocence.
Her brothers took her with them, promising an "adventure"
in exchange for the nickel she'd been given to buy a hamburger.
She hid her eyes; she was only eight years old.

At what cost a life?

Here the television—that simulacrum—our witness
to debates over *high tech lynching*
flickers equivalences/ the nightly news.
Or that photo-opt in the *Illustrated Book of African American
History*: a charred body swaying, white faces clustered round
blotting out the singed background. All smiles.

She crossed a lane, no signal. Later, plastic bags, marijuana residue,
and pride to boot. *A wise ass savvy black women ain't
takin' no talk from whitey boy* (or so he projected).
But later we see in the cam shots one gorgeous, lean
swaying woman. Off camera— you were dragged—
we hear your voice in the handcuffed take-down.

Have we eaten of that tree again,
but with neither knowledge nor innocence
to show for it? Simple witness
the weakest of things?

At what cost a life?

You are in my orchard tonight, Sandra,
along with the clever foxes.
Imaginary gardens with real toads in them
—that's what the poet said.

She (Un)Names Them

Sandhill cranes—
a trill at 5,000 feet

coyote scat, their tracks too

feral pigs powder the earth
their rootings here and there

Audubon distinguishes for her:
a Wilson's warbler from a yellow-rumped one.

She names them.

Once she was called *Baby Allison*
but only for a month

until adopting parents arrived.

They named her *Shelley* after a great grandfather
himself named for a family friend, Percy Bysshe

Now this: she discovers through an intermediary,
required by the state, her mother's name

and a living member of her DNA family
a half-brother, a *Proffitt*

She would like to read things this way:
Proffitt from Scottish, English, and French origins

someone gifted with the ability to see the future
that would go nicely with Allison (from Alice in Greek meaning truth)

After all, the no name putative father
revealed he was married then disappeared

They name her.

But is she any of these—so much water
and blood under the bridge.

Even her favorite, Shelley, *a dweller
on the clearing near the meadow*

speaks silence to what was once
trill, grunt, song.

Blue Heron

1.
It's your shadow I seek
cool mystery.

2.
I stood once, in a natural history museum
under a California condor,
stuffed, exhibited, a cautionary note
as eggs somewhere nearby
were carefully protected until hatched—
the young to be released and tracked
in the wild.
Now that was a shadow.

3.
But yours, the briefest greyness
shift of Rio Grande light

4.
To address animals
in the 21st century
is to ignore
the reality of cyberspace,
the virtual penumbra
and even
Plato's legacy—perhaps?

5.
But still I come looking for you
and more: a habit of landscape
which says *continuity,*
which countenances the four-wheeler ruts
and your silence,
your disappearing act.

6.
To compensate:
Elegant simplicity,
like a sharp penciled stroke,
from the crown of your rounded head
down, one grey movement.

7.
To admit to the art of you
without stinging flies
or gnats, skyward.

8.
We could never be that close
—to appreciate your mundaneness—
without stuffing you.

9.
There must be a nest on the bosque side
of the river, so developed in its bike trails
and horse farms.
You ignore barking dogs,
the exhaust fumes from nearby suburban streets,
in flight.

10.
And why not?
My feet are cold,
my socks are in the dryer.
It's rainy today,
not a day for hunting shadows.
A day completed in shadow.

11.
I've been told
you stubbornly stay
in your favorite pond
even in winter
even sometimes as the ice forms

around your stilts for legs.
In a surprise season
you risk being
frozen in place
O fisherman.

12.
Lord of stillness
you proofread hunger.
You make a habit
of reverence.

13.
As far as I know
you are no
totem bird.
But who cares?
This is no reality show.

14.
Like the fish
I come in seeming safety
under the shadow
of your wing.
Perhaps like them,
the instant before you
pluck them up,
maybe the instant
before they're swallowed
my heart skitters
at the promise
of a death so still.

15.
Memory, like shadow,
holds fast
inverts its original.

16.

So still as to fool
our casual walk.

17.
Almost past, heads down
we pause in our conversation.
And you, there on the sand bank,
focus on the waters around you,
island below.

18.
And us.

19.
I get up,
eat dry cherrios.
I look for my glasses.
I think of a walk
down by the river.

20.
What worlds of yours
do we inhabit—
neither your careless frogs
nor beguiled fishes?
I know you will eat
anything to stay alive.

21.
Elegant simplicity:
like a sharp-penciled stroke,
from the crown of your rounded head
down.
One grey movement.

22.
Somewhere your secret nest.
Somewhere your shadow sits.

Acknowledgments

Counting Cattle with the Fathers, *Five New Mexico Poets*
Blue Heron, *Tiny Seed*
Plainsong, *An Anthology of New Mexico Poets*
Antelope and I, *Spiral Orb*
Friendship, *Texas Poetry Assignment*
Languages Lost, *Unknotting the Line: The Prose in Poetry*, anthology edited by David Weischen and Scott Wiggerman
Removal, *Unknotting the Line: The Prose in Poetry,* anthology edited by David Weischen and *Scott Wiggerman*

I am so grateful to teachers, family, and friends who listened, suggested, cared. Special thanks to sage mentor and guide, Juliet Patterson, to BK Loren who believed in the lyric in prose and poetry, to friends Gail Hovey and Genneil Curphy for tolerating early drafts, and to teachers Joy Harjo and Aimee Nezhukumatathil for your inspiration. And to the Wurlitzer Foundation where this project modestly began and Writing Workshops in Greece where it caught sail.

Shelley Armitage, professor, writer, naturalist, lives in the Chihuahuan desert in Las Cruces, New Mexico. She is author of eight award-winning books, including *John Held, Jr.: Illustrator of the Jazz Age, The World of Rose O'Neill,* and *The Pajarito Journals of Peggy Pond Church. Walking the Llano, A Texas Memoir of Place* was a *Kirkus* starred book cited as one of the best memoirs of the year, and a finalist for the May Sarton prize, the New Mexico-Arizona book awards, and the Collins P. Carr award from the Texas Institute of Letters.

Armitage has won the Southwest Book Award and the Emily Toth award and was a finalist for the Eudora Welty Prize and the Indies Book of the Year. Her work has been featured on National Public Radio and has appeared in such works as *True Border, Shifting Views and Changing Places: the Photographs of Rick Dingus, Multicultural America, the Southwest Review, The Post-2000 Western, Projecting Words: Writing Images.* Among her honors are a fellowship from the Wurlitzer Foundation, a Distinguished Chair in American Literature Fulbright in Warsaw, Fulbright awards in Finland and Portugal, a National Endowment for the Arts grant, three National Endowment for the Humanities grants, and a Rockefeller grant. She is professor emerita at the University of Texas at El Paso where she held the Roderick Chair and is a member of the Texas Institute of Letters.

Armitage participates in various conservation practices including New Mexico Site Watch and Tree Stewards. She has been recognized by the US Department of Agriculture for management of her family grasslands near Vega, Texas. She finds inspiration there of how the power of landscape draws us into a greater understanding of ourselves and others as we experience kinship with the places we inhabit.

www.ingramcontent.com/pod-product-compliance
Lightning Source LLC
Chambersburg PA
CBHW020343170426
43200CB00006B/481